U0781868

# COMMERCIAL ACTIVITIES
# 商务活动

《中国商务文化》编写组

北京语言大学出版社
BEIJING LANGUAGE AND CULTURE
UNIVERSITY PRESS

中央广播电视大学音像出版社
MULTIMEDIA PRESS, OPEN UNIVERSITY OF CHINA

总 监 制：戚德祥　梁小庆

监　　制：张　健　魏　捷

顾　　问：周小华

主　　编：李孚嘉

编　　者：李佳琳　唐琪佳　王墨妍　张维嘉
　　　　　（按音序排列）

英文翻译：巩　熠　罗正鹏　孙齐圣

英文审定：【美】Andrew Bauer　李亚婉

# 目 录 CONTENTS

# 接待中国来访者
## RECEIVING VISITORS FROM CHINA

《论语》里有句话:"有朋自远方来,不亦乐乎?"中国人热情好客,对远道而来、久未谋面的朋友更是热情。那么,怎样能接待好远道而来的中国商务伙伴呢?

In *The Analects of Confucius*, the Master said, "Isn't it a pleasure to have friends coming from afar?" The Chinese people enjoy hospitality and entertain with more warmth the coming of long-lost friends from afar. So then the question becomes how to treat Chinese business partners from afar?

在商务交往中，接待是不可忽视的一个环节，它对合作双方建立关系、开展合作都有重要的影响。周到的接待可以给客人留下良好的印象，有助于商务交往的展开。

迎接客人是接待工作的第一步。中国人讲究"笑迎远客"，这里的"迎"有距离和方式的差别，一般由访客地位的高低及双方关系的亲疏决定。如果是重要的本地客人或是初次到访的外地客人，主人一般会到大门口或楼下迎接；对于一般的客人，主人只需在办公室或会议室等待即可。如果是级别较高的客人从外地来访，主人会

派与其级别相当的人去机场、码头或车站迎接；但如果客人此行的目的不止一个，双方的会晤只是行程中的一部分，客人可能已经下榻宾馆，主人则会派专车去宾馆迎接。因此，在制订接待方案时，主人除了了解对方到达的时间、人员名单外，确认来访人员的身份、了解对方的行程安排等也非常重要，这样才能确保迎接工作万无一失。

中国有句古语"迎来送往"，与迎客对应的便是送客。作为接待工作的最后环节，送客的意义可能比迎客还要重要，因为最初的印象可以在访问期间弥补，而最后的印象近期很少有机会再改变。因此，"善始"还要"善终"，送客的方式应与迎客方式一致，迎多远就应送多远，才不会让客人有心理落差。比如，如果在接待中安排了接机的环节，就一定要在客人走时安排送机。

除了迎送之外，客人来访期间的日程安排也要在接待之前制订好。中国人的做客之道是"客随主便"，因此主人会更多地为客人着想，将客人的行程安排得非常充实。除了洽谈工作外，其他时间主人会为客人安排许多休闲活动，比如带客人去游览本地

In business intercourse, reception of your partners is a link that can never be ignored, as it will influence building relationships between partners and carrying out success in future cooperation. A good reception will impress the visitors and help start up the business.

To greet guests is the first step. In China, meeting visitors with a smile is emphasized. Also, the way of greeting and venue to meet guests usually depend on the status of the visitors and the degree of their closeness. For important local visitors or first time non-local visitors in China, the host will generally go downstairs to meet them or greet them at the front door. In general visitors, the host will wait by the door of the office or meeting room. If the important visitors come from other regions, the host may ask an employee of similar position to greet the counterpart at the airport, port or the train station. However, if the visitors intend to visit more than one company, and the meeting between the two sides is only one part of their trip, the Chinese visitors may prefer to go to the hotel on their own. The host will arrange for a private particular vehicle to pick them up at the hotel. To summarize, the host should, when planning for meeting the visitors, not only be aware of the time of their arrival and their names, but of their positions and schedules. It is very important to get these aspects of information in advance to assure the success of the meeting.

An old Chinese saying says, "welcome visitors and see them off". In other words, as the last step of treating visitors, seeing off is probably more important than greeting, because the first impression could be changed during the visit, but the final impression can hardly be changed. Therefore, a good beginning should accompany a better ending. For example, if the visitor was greeted at the airport, he should be seen off by someone all the way to the airport as well.

Besides the greeting and seeing off, the detailed arrangements for the whole visit should be made before visitors arrive. The Chinese way of treating visitors demands meeting the needs of the visitors. So, the host should consider from the visitors' perspective when arranging a full program that includes both formal business meetings and social visits

的特色景点、品尝当地美食等。很多活动甚至是主人利用周末或晚上的私人时间陪同客人。中国人认为，在有限的时间内，多看一些东西、多接触一些人，才能较好地实现出访的价值。如果活动安排得太少，会让客人在宾馆无所事事，感觉受到冷遇。主人在有限的时间内与客人多接触，可增进彼此的了解，也有利于建立亲密的人际关系，商务交往会因此事半功倍。

饮食在日程安排中也很重要。不同的国家，饮食习惯有较大差异。在安排就餐时，除了请中国客人品尝当地美食之外，安排一两次中餐是很有必要的，这样可以照顾一下他们的"中国胃"，避免因饮食习惯不同而引发胃口不适。另外，绝大多数中国人不习惯吃冷食、喝冰水，因此一定要注意食物及饮品的温度。为他们准备随时可以饮用的热水是非常周到的一种做法。

成功的接待工作可以让来访者感受到合作的诚意，双方由此建立信任，从而促进商务活动的顺利开展。

such as cultural sightseeing and local food tasting. Sometimes, the host may even spend his or her private time, like evenings and weekends, escorting the guests around. It is a common thinking for the Chinese people that the value of a visit to a new place could be achieved only by seeing more and communicating more within a limited time. If the host does not arrange more events for the visitors, the guests may feel being left out in the cold by staying in the hotel for such a long time. Spending more time together could help to establish better understanding and closer personal relationships between the host and visitors. This will also lead to smooth business intercourse in the near future.

The arrangement of the meals is very important as well. As dietary habits vary greatly from country to country, it is necessary to invite the guests to try some delicious local cuisines, and the better way is to arrange one or two Chinese meals during the visit. This can help take care of their "appetite" and avoid the discomfort caused by eating exotic food. In addition, most Chinese people are not used to cold food and cold water, so the host should always pay attention to the temperature of the food and drinks. It is a considerate behavior to serve hot water at any time.

A successful treating can allow the visitors to feel the sincerity of the host for cooperation and build up the mutual trust needed to open the door for business activities.

**国 案例**

　　老刘是一家中国公司的副总裁，一次他带领考察团到美国中部的一座城市考察潜在合作企业的生产经营情况，商讨合作事宜。考察团于美国时间周五傍晚抵达，发现只有一辆出租车在机场等待他们。随后考察团被带到一家宾馆休息，并被告知晚上自行去宾馆餐厅用餐。周六、周日整整两天，美方没有人与考察团联系。由于对环境不熟悉，并且宾馆较为偏远、交通不便，周末两天考察团只能待在宾馆。周一上午，美国企业再次用出租车接考察团去参观工厂，下午安排商务洽谈。访问活动一结束，第二天考察团就立刻启程回国，最终也没有与美国企业签约合作。

**点评**　美国企业在接待过程中忽略了几个细节：第一，没有派专人专车到机场接机；第二，没有安排欢迎晚宴；第三，没有安排丰富的行程。以上这几点使中国考察团感觉被冷落了，认为这次出行没有受到美方的重视，美方没有合作的诚意，这直接影响了双方的合作。

## 📖 CASE STUDY

Mr. Liu is the vice President of a Chinese company. He once led a delegation to investigate the production and operation of a potential cooperative enterprise located in a city in the middle of the US, intending to discuss potential cooperation with that company. When the delegation arrived in the US in the evening (local time) on a Friday, they found that there was only one taxi waiting for them at the airport. The delegation was brought to a hotel and was informed to have dinner at the hotel's restaurant on their own. For the following two weekend days, no one from the US enterprise contacted the delegation. The delegation stayed at the hotel which was in a remote area with no public transportation. They had to stay there for the whole weekend because they had no idea how to go around the city. On Monday morning, the enterprise arranged a taxi to pick them up for a site visit of the production line in the factory, followed by a business meeting in the afternoon. Just after the visit, the delegation left the US the following day and in the end they did not sign any contract with this US enterprise.

📎 Comments: The US enterprise omitted several details during the whole visit. First, the enterprise arranged no employees or cars to pick up the delegation. Second, it didn't offer a welcome dinner. Third, it didn't arrange any social events. Consequently, the Chinese delegation felt left out and ignored by the US side. They thought the US enterprise lacked sincere intentions for the cooperation, which directly affected the potential cooperation between the two companies.

## ◎ 行动指南

- 接待者在机场、车站或者码头迎接来访者时应注意一定要提前到达，否则会给人留下失职和不守时的印象。双方见面后，接待方负责人应主动将迎宾人员姓名、职务一一介绍给来访者。

- 在接待过程中注意一些细节可以给来访者留下好印象。比如，接待者帮助来访者办理领取托运行李的手续，为来访者准备一些本地的报纸或旅游指南，提前为来访者安排好住宿，出行安排专车接送。

## ⊘ ADVICE

● The host should arrive at the airport, train station or port in advance. Otherwise, they might leave on the visitors an impression that the host is not fulfilling the duty and not being punctual. When the visitors meet the host for the first time, the head of the hosting party should introduce his or her colleagues to the visitors with their name and position.

● Paying attention to the details during the reception will leave a good impression on the visitors. For instance, the staff of the hosting party could help the visitors have their luggage checked-in, prepare local newspapers or a tourist guide, confirm accommodation and arrange special transport for them.

# 家中接待来访者
## RECEIVING GUESTS AT HOME

在中国，客人对主人的最高评价是"热情好客"，那么，怎样做才算是"热情好客"呢？

Introduction: In China, The highest compliment given by a guest to describe a host is "warm and welcoming". But what do these words really mean in China?

汉语中"好客"一词的意思是热诚大方地接待、款待客人，乐意与之分享食物或住处。在中国传统文化中，早有对主人和客人的行为规约，它们分别是"主随客意"和"客随主便"。我们可以发现它们有一个共同的汉字——"随"，它是成为一个受欢迎的客人或一个合格的主人的关键所在。"随"的意思是"顺从，不违背"。这就要求主人按照客人的意思来进行安排，或者客人依随主人的安排行事。这两种做法都需要从对方的意愿着想来进行考虑和安排。

作为主人，他的义务是让客人有舒适的感觉，让客人在主人家却感觉像在自己家里一样惬意、舒适，不拘束，这是主人的最高追求；作为客人，要尽量不给主人添麻烦，因为一旦提出某些要求，就意味着主人会尽量满足，可能会打乱主人原来的安排，增加不必要的麻烦。所以，在接待中国客人时可能会出现这样的情况：客人到来后，主人询问客人喝什么，客人会说"随便"、"都行"。针对主人的询问，客人没有作出具体的回应，而是让主人以"方便"为原则为他准备任意一种饮品即可。有的客人甚至会说"别忙了"、"我不渴"来委婉地拒绝主人。面对这种回应，主人一般都不会就此罢休，而是继续提出新的建议，比如"给您泡一杯茶吧，我新买的，您尝尝"，或"天太热，给

In Chinese, "Hao ke" literally means treating the guests warmly and generously and being happy to share food and residence with them. Rules of conduct made for hosts and guests can be found in the traditional Chinese culture, namely, "Zhu Sui Ke Yi (the host must do as his guest wishes)" and "Ke Sui Zhu Bian (the guest must suit the convenience of the host)". It can be found that the two phrases contain the same Chinese character "Sui", which is the key criterion for being a popular guest or a good host. "Sui" literally means "be obedient to or abide by". That is to say, both the guest and the host should consider and arrange things from each other's perspective.

For the host, it is the duty to make the guests feel comfortable. The highest pursuit of the host is to make the guest feel just at home. Being the guest, he/she will do his/her best not to bring the host any trouble. Once he/she makes special requests, the host may try to fulfill his/her demands by disrupting the original plan and some troubles may occur. While treating Chinese guests, you may encounter the following situation: the host asks the guests what they want to drink when they sit down, and the guests tend to say "any drink you have" or "anything". Actually, rather than make specific requests, Chinese guests prefer to let the host choose a drink at his/her convenience. Some guests may even say "I can take care of myself" or "I am not thirsty" to politely decline the drinks. Generally, hearing these responses, the host would not stop asking but continue raising new suggestions, such as "May I make a cup of tea for you? I just bought some tea. Would you like to try some?" or "It's too hot today, do you want a glass of ice water?" At this time, most guests would say

您拿杯冰水吧"。这时客人大多是不会拒绝的，除非他确实不能喝某种饮品。面对客人的拒绝，主人不妨多让几次，如果客人拒绝了三次以上，那么就放弃吧，因为"主随客意"嘛！

在家庭招待中，宴请占有重要的地位。中国家庭在招待客人时，主人的家庭成员常有不同的分工。比如夫妻两人接待客人时，一方会负责招待客人，陪他们聊天儿，另一方则在厨房准备饭菜。中国的宴请至少要上七八道菜，有的地方有"四冷四热"之说，即四个凉菜、四个热菜。如果是丰盛的宴会，热菜可能更多。饭菜的品种和数量越多，越能表现主人的好客；越名贵、越奇特的菜越能显示主人的殷勤和客人的身份。当然，如果饭菜数量不够，客人也会有意不吃饱，给主人留下一些在盘子里，不致让主人感到尴尬，大不了回家后再补一顿。因此，招待中国客人时，多准备一些食物，多做几个菜，会让客人感受到主人的欢迎和热情，主客之间的关系会更亲密。

吃饱喝足，聊得尽兴了，客人便会知趣地向主人告别。这时，客人会站起来说"时候不早了，我们该走了"，或者说"今天让你们受累了，我们告辞了"。主人和客人离开客厅后走至门口可能还要再聊一会儿，然后客人才真正告别。一般情况下，主人要陪同客人走到电梯口甚至楼门口；如果客人是开车来的，主人还会把客人送到汽车旁，等客人开车离去后才转身走开。更殷勤的做法是，主人会一直目送客人离开，直至看不见客人的身影才转身回去。如果主人把客人送到门口后很快就关门，会使客人有突兀感，是不礼貌的。

一次好的招待会给客人留下良好的印象，对朋友关系的建立、合作的开展非常有帮助。在客人到来前准备充足的食品和饮料，客人到来后热情地陪伴，客人离开时殷勤地"远送"，这些都是"好客"的主人应该做到的。

"yes" unless he or she cannot drink certain drinks for health reasons. Even though the guests may decline the drink, the host will repeat his/her offer again and again. Yet, please give up your offer if the guest declines three times, because the host must do as his guest wishes.

For family hosting, the dinner plays an important role. The family members have different roles when hosting the guests. For example, if the host is a couple, one of them will talk with the guests, while the other will prepare food in the kitchen. There are at least seven or eight dishes in a Chinese family dinner. There is a saying: "four cold

ones and four hot ones", which means the dinner should have four cold dishes and four hot dishes. If the number of guests is large, more hot dishes will be served. The Chinese tend to offer a lot of food, far more than the amount that the host and the guest can eat. It is thought that the more the food is served, and the greater the variety is, the more welcoming the host is. The more expensive and special the dish is, the more honor and respect will be shown to the guest. If the food is not enough, the Chinese guests will pretend to be full and leave some on the plates so as not to embarrass the host even though they may need to have more to eat upon returning home. It is better to prepare more food and serve more dishes in order to make the guests feel the welcoming and the hospitality of the host. This will all also make the host and guests closer.

After a rich meal and a really nice conversation, the guests will know it's time to leave. At that time, the guests will stand up and say "it's getting late, so we have to go" or "you are so tired today, we are going to leave." Sometimes, after leaving the dining room, the host

国 **案例**

　　小王去 John 家做客。John 非常热情地招待了小王，两人聊得也很开心。小王告辞后没走多远，发现自己的手表落在了洗手间里，他折返回来按了门铃。John 从门镜中看到是小王后打开了门，但只是开了一道缝，问清了来意后 John 没有让小王再次进门，而是让小王在门外等，John 拿来手表从门缝中递给了小王，整个过程中小王只见到了 John 的半张脸。虽然拿回了东西，但小王留下了很不愉快的印象，接受款待时的温馨顿时荡然无存。

✎**点评**　　开门只留道门缝与客人交谈是不礼貌的。客人不能和主人面对面交流，难免心生不快。尽管小王对之前的拜访很满意，但后来的折返没有受到礼遇，John 的款待"功亏一篑"。

and guest may talk for a while at the door, and then the guest will leave. Generally, guests will not only be accompanied to the elevator, but also to the first floor entrance. If the guest leaves with his/her own car, the host will not only walk with the visitor to the parking lot, but also wait next to his car until he leaves. What's more, the host may even see off the guests until they cannot be seen anymore. In China, the guests may feel the host is abrupt and insincere if the host only escorts the guests to the door and closes the door immediately after their leaving.

A good hosting will leave a good impression on the guests, and it's very helpful to develop friendship and start to carry out cooperations with the guests. It is a duty for a good host to prepare sufficient food and drinks before the guests arrive, accompany them with enthusiasm and see them off far.

## 📖 CASE STUDY

Xiao Wang visited John's home as a guest. John treated him very warmly and they chatted very happily. When Xiao Wang left the house and hadn't gone far, he found he had left his watch in the washroom so he went back to John's house and rang the bell. John looked through the peephole and then opened the door. But the door just opened a crack and John didn't let Xiao Wang come in. Instead, he asked what he needs and told him to wait. Then, he got the watch and gave it to Xiao Wang through the crack. In the whole process, Xiao Wang only saw half of the face of John. Although he got his watch back, he became quite unhappy with John and the good time in John's home was completely spoiled.

📎 Comments: It is rude to crack open the door and speak with guests in Chinese culture. The Chinese guests would be unhappy as the host did not speak with them face to face and treated them like thieves. In Wang's case, although he was satisfied with the visit at the beginning, the impolite behaviors of John ruined everything in the end.

## ⊘ 行动指南

● 中国人做客时可能会对某些物品感兴趣，询问它们的价格，这时请不要觉得被冒犯。客人可能仅仅出于好奇，或想通过对物品的赞扬表达这样一个隐含的意思——拥有这样东西的主人非常有眼光。面对这样的问题，如果不方便回答可以给一个模糊的回答，比如"一千多块吧"，或者让客人猜价格，或者干脆岔开话题。

● 中国人在宴请中一般都是在餐桌上饮酒，在饭后没有饮酒的习惯。饭后可能还会给客人换上新沏的茶，或者用水果作为饭后的消遣。

## ⊘ ADVICE

- Chinese guests may show interests in some items and ask the price of them. Don't be offended when the Chinese people do so because they are either only curious about them or trying to say that the owner has good tastes by praising the items. If you don't want to tell the price, just say a rough number, like "it's about 1000 RMB", or let the guest take a guess or change the subject as you like.

- Chinese people usually drink alcohol during the banquets rather than after the meals. After the meal, the host may serve tea for the guest or provide fruits as dessert.

# 办公室的东道主
# BEING A HOST IN AN OFFICE

中国人注重"礼尚往来",意思是在礼节上有来有往。中国人在接待客人的时候热情有加,因此他们也期待自己在拜访主人时能受到同样的礼遇。如何在办公室做好东道主呢?

Chinese people think highly of a saying that "etiquette requires reciprocity", which means you should deal with other people as politely as they deal with you. When hosting guests, they will be very welcoming, and they expect the same courteous reception as well. So, how to be a good host of an office visit?

中国人热情好客，讲究待客之道，如果你想在办公室做一个热情好客的东道主，应该留意这样几个环节：

首先是迎客。在商务场合，迎客有级别差异，讲究地位对等。对于非常重要的客人，接待方同级别的人最好下楼或出门去迎接；如果对来访者非常重视，接待方还应有更高级别的领导出面接见，表示欢迎。如果来访团领导的级别很高，接待方除了有最高领导出席，其他各部门负责人最好也出席欢迎仪式。接待方尽可能地展现对访客的重视和诚意，会使后续的洽谈更加顺利。

其次是待客。在接待中国客人时，不得不提"茶"。中国人有来客奉茶的习俗。俗话说："来客不敬茶，不

是好人家。"奉茶能表达出主人热情友好、诚挚尊敬的心意，从而在宾主之间营造出温暖快乐的交往氛围。在中国，茶的种类繁多，茶具也各式各样，且有等级之分。一般主人会根据客人的身份挑选与之匹配的茶和茶具，越是贵客越是要用好茶叶和好茶具来招待，否则会被视为不敬。

待客斟茶的时候，要掌握时机和分寸。在客人喝去一多半时就应及时添加开水，使茶汤浓度、温度前后大体一致。斟茶时不可斟满，七分即可。太满让客人不好端，溢出了茶水，不但浪费，也会烫着客人的手或泼到衣服上，另外还寓意希望客人赶快离开。因此，中国有句话叫"从来茶道七分满，留下三分是人情"。这也是中国人的处世之道，意思是"做人不要做绝，说话不要说尽"，要懂得为自己、为别人留有余地。"水满则溢，月盈则亏"，凡事都能留有余地，才可避免走向极端。

最后是时间。在中国，赴约早到

In China, people have their own way to show hospitality and warmth. If someone is invited to your office and you want to be a good host, attention should be paid to the following steps:

First comes the greeting of the guests. In business activities, the guests are divided into several levels according to their status. For very important visitors, the host would ask an employee of similar position to go downstairs or go out to greet them. For more important visitors, the host would arrange a leader of higher status to welcome them outside the office. If the head of the delegation is very powerful, not only the top leader of the hosting party but also the heads of other departments would attend the welcoming ceremony. In sum, the host should do his best to show his sincerity and hospitality, which would help the following negotiations go on well. It is an etiquette in China to "welcome visitors and see them off" in the same way. The host should always remember to see the guests off as warmly as the very beginning. Otherwise, the guests may feel ignored in the end.

The second step is entertaining the guests. When entertaining a Chinese guest, you should never forget the tea because it is a custom in China. As the Chinese saying goes, "A family serving no tea to the guests is not a good family". By showing hospitality, sincerity and respect while serving tea, the relationship between the host and guests is strengthened in a friendly atmosphere. There are a large variety of tea and tea sets in China. All the tea and tea sets are graded. When the guests come, the host would choose a proper tea and tea set according to their status. The higher the status is, the better the tea and tea set the host would choose. If you make a bad choice, it will be regarded as a sign of disrespect.

When serving tea, you should pay attention to the timing and the amount of the water. When the tea

很高，一般不会早到，会准点赴约。

在中国，你可能会遇到事先没有预约的"不速之客"。不速之客突然拜访，有可能是客人碰巧在附近办事，想顺道拜访主人。不速之客也有可能是与主人关系较为亲近的人，没有预约，只是时机合适便登门拜访。面对不速之客，你别太介意，可凭自己的安排决定是否接待他们，毕竟这样的客人并不多见。但是对关系亲近的客人的突然拜访，中国人一般都会放下手头的事情去亲自接待，并且留给客人的时间相对宽松。在中国人眼里，人际关系的维护远比恪守日程表更加重要。不过，现在绝大多数中国人在拜访之前都会提前预约，办理越重要的事情、拜访越重要的人，提前预约的时间越长。

不为失礼。一般而言，客人如果越重视这次会面或者要见的人越重要，他们会到得越早，宁可自己等主人，也不要主人等自己。早到的客人，有的会在附近逗留一阵，等到接近约定时间再去拜访主人；有的则会直奔目的地，如果此刻你不方便接待，可以让客人在会客室等一会儿，不一定要打乱原有的时间安排。如果客人的级别

has run half, it's time for you to pour more hot water for the guests. If you don't pour water in time, the tea will not be as hot and strong as the very beginning. You should pour the cup about 7/10 full rather than 10/10 full. If the cup is too full, it would be difficult for the guests to hold. If the tea overflows the cup, not only the tea will be wasted, the guest's hands may also be hurt from the hot water or their clothes and may get wet. Remember that a full cup of tea means the guests are not welcome in the house. The Chinese saying "always pour the tea cup 7/10 full in order to do a favor for the guest" tells the Chinese philosophy of life. It means that you should be moderate and should never say absolute words. You should always leave room for yourself and the guests. As another Chinese saying goes, "the moon waxes only to wane; water brims only to overflow". Only by leaving space for everything can you avoid going to extremes.

The last thing is time. Chinese people have a relatively flexible timetable. When you greet them, it's not necessary to take time too seriously. For the Chinese, it doesn't matter whether the guest arrives five minutes early or late. What really matters is whether the things can go well and whether the expecting goal can be achieved. Besides, it's not rude to arrive early in China. Generally speaking, the more important the meeting is or the host is, the earlier the guests will arrive. They would rather wait for the host than let the host wait for them. If they arrive early, some of them would hang around for a few minutes until the appointed time. Others may greet the host without hesitation. If you are too busy to meet the guests, you can let them wait in the meeting room instead of changing your own schedule. If the guests rank very high, in general, they would arrive just in time.

As mentioned before, Chinese people don't always follow the schedule. Sometimes, you may encounter some uninvited guests. They might go to a nearby place for work and want to take this chance to visit you. Perhaps they are close to you and just want to see you when they have time (although they didn't make an appointment). If this occurs, you can decide whether to greet them by yourself as an unexpected visit. After all, such a

▣ 案例

　　Jack 是一家澳大利亚公司驻中国的代表。有一天，他在办公室接到一位中国客户小张的电话："你好，Jack，我现在在你们公司附近办事，如果你有时间，半个小时后我能不能过去跟你谈谈改进后的产品设计？你看我们也隔得挺远的，今天碰巧过来了，正好能顺道把事都办了。"半个小时后，Jack 勉强接待了小张，但是心里不太高兴，因为原定的时间安排被这位不速之客打乱了。Jack 根本无心洽谈，最后，会面只好匆匆结束，小张也没有实现预想的效果。

✎ **点评**　　如果遇到了不速之客，他们其实无意非要打乱你的时间计划，而只是问问看，是否你的时间也如此凑巧。如果你的时间安排已经满了，并且不希望计划被打乱，如实拒绝他们的拜访也不算失礼。

case is seldom. However, if the Chinese know the visitors quite well, they would always stop working and host them on their own, and give enough time for them. The reason is that Chinese will stop working and host them not only on their own, but also let them stay as long as they wish. It is a common thinking in China that maintaining interpersonal relationships is much more important than following the schedule. But now, most Chinese people would make a reservation in advance. They may meet a person and deal with an issue. The more important the issue is, and the more important the person is, the earlier the reservation should be made.

## 📖 CASE STUDY

Jack works in China as the representative of an Australian company. One day, he got a phone call in his office. It was from a Chinese customer, Xiao Zhang, "Hi, Jack! I went out for work today and I'm around your company right now. If you have time, can I meet you in half an hour? I think we can talk about the improved design of the product. You know, our companies are so far apart. And I happened to be somewhere near your company, so I really hope that we can meet today." Half an hour later, Jack reluctantly greeted Xiao Zhang, and he was quite unhappy because the unexpected guest turned his arrangements upside down. At that time, Jack had no desires to continue the discussion. In the end, the meeting ceased in a hurry, and Xiao Zhang didn't realize his desired outcomes.

📎 Comments: If you encounter some unexpected guests, remember that they do not want to interrupt your schedules, but to ask whether you happen to have some time to meet them. If you don't have time and don't want to change the schedule, it's not rude to refuse them.

## ⊘ 行动指南

- 中国人习惯喝热茶，不要用没有煮沸的水冲泡茶叶，否则会被认为是无意待客，没有礼貌。

- 招待重要、尊贵的客人，别用一次性纸杯泡茶。一次性纸杯虽然方便，却可能被认为不够尊敬。

- 放置茶壶时壶嘴不能正对他人，否则表示请人赶快离开。

## ⊘ ADVICE

● The Chinese are used to drinking hot tea. You will be regarded as an insincere and impolite person if you don't use boiling water to make tea.

● Don't use disposable paper cups when serving tea to the important and distinguished guest. Although these cups are convenient, the guest would feel disrespected.

● Should you ever handle a teapot, remember not to put it down with the spout pointing at anyone: this means that person (the one being pointed at) is not welcome in the house.

# 办公室的访问者
## BEING A VISITOR IN AN OFFICE

中国有句话叫"无事不登三宝殿"，意思是没有事不会登门造访。当你要去拜访客户时，一定"有事相求"。如何做好办公室的访问者，顺利达成你的拜访目的呢？

There is a saying in China that "never go to the temple for nothing", which means you wouldn't visit someone if you don't have something to ask of him. If you are going to visit a client, you must want something from him. The following paragraphs will tell you how to visit a Chinese client in the office and how to achieve your goals.

中国人比较注重人际关系，因此，拜访时人际关系的准备是不可忽视的一环。一般而言，如果你初次拜访某位中国客户，最好有其他人的引见。他人的引见可以比较容易打破人际关系的信任壁垒，使沟通变得更加顺畅。引见人与客户的关系越亲密，被引见人取得合作成功的机会便越大。

被人引见之后，就要预约见面的时间。通常级别越高、越繁忙的客户需要提前预约的时间越长，这样显得更加郑重与重视。如果是拜访关系很密切的老客户，提前预约的时间可以缩短，即使最后一分钟通知对方，对方可能也会接受和欢迎。尽管偶尔会

遇到不速之客，但是随着人们生活和工作节奏的加快，在中国现代商务交往中，绝大多数人在邀请与会面之前都会提前预约。

极少数情况下，中国人也可能会因为一些突发的重大事件而临时取消约会，在他们心目中，事件重要性是排在时间表之前的，他们会优先处理重要和紧急的事情。一旦约会临时被取消，访问者最好第一时间与客户预约下次见面的时间，这次预约的时间可以缩短，因为客户一般不好意思拒绝。

中国人在拜访他人时，可以接受主人在谈话的同时处理其他紧急的事情，比如看电脑、接电话、发短信，客人能够体恤主人的繁忙，一般都会耐心地等主人处理完着急的事情再继续下面的谈话。这在中国不算是一件失礼的事情，因为他们习惯在同一时间处理好几件事情，认为这样更有效率。主人也可能根据谈话的具体进展而调整会面的时间；会谈时间到了便立刻结束，这在中国人看来不近人情，他们无法接受。如果约定结束的时间到了，但是还有一点儿遗留问题，主人通常不会立刻结束，而是稍微延长一下会谈时间，直到问题

The Chinese people think that the interpersonal relationships is pretty important. Before meeting the host, it's necessary to find some ways to build a relationship with him. In your initial approach, it's best to find an intermediary and go through him. If you come with someone known to the Chinese clients, you will be trusted more easily and the negotiation will advance more smoothly. The deeper the relationship between the intermediary and the client, the bigger the chance is you have to do business with the host.

If you can find an intermediary, it's time to make an appointment through him/her. Generally, the more powerful the client is, the earlier the reservation should be made. Because this will make the client feel well treated and respected. To meet regular customers, it's not necessary to make a reservation that early. Even if you contact the client at the last minute, he would be happy to meet you. Long before, Chinese people often visited a friend without calling. If a guest suddenly showed up at the front door, the host would let him in cheerfully. As the pace of life and work sped up, however, it's necessary to make an appointment for a meeting or a visit in advance when doing business in modern China.

Chinese people may welcome uninvited guests, but they may cancel the scheduled appointments unexpectedly. So you should be well prepared for a sudden cancellation and remember that Chinese people may change the schedule as necessary. Rather than stick to the schedule, they focus more on the participants and the result. For example, they would cancel the appointment when they meet some emergencies. In their mind, the order of work is determined by its importance, so the most important and urgent work would be done first. Once the appointment is canceled by a Chinese client, you should find another time to meet him. This time, there is no need to contact him as early as the first time because he would feel too sorry to disappoint you again.

As mentioned before, Chinese people are pretty flexible. If a host speak with the Chinese guest and do other things at the same time, such as looking at the computer, answering phones or sending texts, the Chinese guests will show great

说"有机会再聊"、"有空常来坐坐"之类，这并非是正式的邀请，而只是一种客套话，因为没有约定具体的时间和地点，你也大可不必太认真，只需回应"一定一定"就可以了。如果你真的想再次登门拜访，那还是要像从前一样提前预约。随着拜访次数的增多，你与主人的关系会越来越密切，在拜访中所受的约束将越来越少，拜访会越来越顺利，因为你开始与主人建立了"关系"。在中国，密切的人际关系是重要的合作基础。

解决；如果遗留的问题还比较多，无法在短时间内全部解决，那么主人会建议另约时间。

拜访结束后，主人可能出于礼貌

understanding and will wait patiently for the host to finish his urgent work. It's not an offensive act in China because they are used to handling several things at the same time. Actually, it is considered as a way to achieve greater efficiency. The host may also adjust the length of the negotiation according to its progress. It seems unreasonable and impolite to end the negotiation strictly according to the timetable. If it's time to put an end to the meeting, but there's still something to be discussed, the host would not end it immediately, but extend it a little bit until the problems are resolved.If there are too many problems and they cannot be solved instantly, the host will suggest another appointment for further discussion.

When you are leaving, the host may say "hope we can meet again", "come and see me sometimes", etc. If he does not mention a specific time and place, you don't need to take it seriously. It's only a courtesy rather than a real invitation. The best answer for this is always "sure, I'd love to". And for the next time, you have to make an appointment in advance just as before. After several visits, you will be closer to the host and a relationship between you and him will be built. Since then, the number of restrictions will begin to decrease and the negotiation will become increasingly successful. Good interpersonal relationships in China lay a solid foundation for cooperation.

**圁 案例**

　　Waltz 是一位家用电器公司的销售经理。为了进一步开拓业务，Waltz 近期一直与一家中国连锁超市的采购部经理刘明积极联系扩大采购的事宜。经过多次邮件和电话沟通，双方形成了初步的合作意向。这一天，Waltz 相约上门拜访刘经理，落实合作事宜。这次会谈很成功，双方相谈甚欢，不仅签订了新的合作协议，Waltz 和刘经理还俨然已经成为了好朋友。会谈结束，告辞的时候，刘经理一边送Waltz出门，一边说："您慢走，有空过来给我们介绍介绍新产品。"Waltz 一听，高兴地问："刘经理，我明天就有空，您方便吗？"却发现刘经理一脸尴尬，说不出话来……

📝**点评** 拜访结束后，刘经理出于礼貌和客气，说"有空过来给我们介绍介绍新产品"，但这并非正式的邀请，只是一种客套话，因为没有约定具体的时间和地点。Waltz 对此过于认真，并急于确定具体的见面时间，这让刘经理很尴尬，既不好意思立刻回绝，更不能随口答应。

## 📰 CASE STUDY

Waltz is a sales manager in a household electric appliance company. Recently, in order to further extend business, Waltz has kept in touch with Liu Ming, a purchasing manager of a chain supermarket in China, to discuss expanding the scale of procurement. The two sides established the initial intention of cooperation after many times of communication through e-mails and telephones. One day, Waltz visited Manager Liu as scheduled and discussed the implementation of cooperative programs with him. The negotiation was a success. The two sides not only had an agreeable conversation, but signed a new cooperation agreement and became good friends at last. After the negotiation, when it was time to say good-bye, Manager Liu saw Waltz off and said, "See you! Please be free to come here and I would be glad to introduce our new products to you." "I'll be free tomorrow. Is that time convenient for you?" Waltz replied with pleasure, but he found that Liu was too embarrassed to say anything.

📝 Comments: Although Manager Liu said "please be free to come here and I would be glad to introduce our new products to you", it is just a polite remark rather than a formal invitation since he didn't mention any specific time and specific place. But Waltz took it too seriously and was too eager to make sure of the meeting time, which embarrassed Liu. So Liu was so embarrassed that he could neither reject it nor make any promise immediately.

### ⊘ 行动指南

● 拜访客户时，要围绕会面的目的有针对性地准备资料，不要仅仅拿着产品彩页和公司宣传画册去拜访客户，最终这些资料总是躺在客户桌子上睡觉。

● 如果会谈是多人交流，提前准备一份交流日程或者交流的问题清单，有助于大家都积极地参与交流。

● 在西方国家一周始于周日，而在中国，则始于周一。因此，在周三的时候，"last Monday"和"next Saturday"在西方指的是本周的周一和周六；但在中国，它们分别指"上周的周一"和"下周的周六"。约定见面时间时要注意。

| Mon | Tue | Wed | Thu | Fri | Sat | Sun |
|-----|-----|-----|-----|-----|-----|-----|
|     |     |     |     |     | 1   | 2   |
| 3   | 4   | 5   | 6   | 7   | 8   | 9   |
| 10  | 11  | 12  | 13  | 14  | 15  | 16  |
| 17  | 18  | 19  | 20  | 21  | 22  | 23  |
| 24  | 25  | 26  | 27  | 28  | 29  | 30  |
| 31  |     |     |     |     |     |     |

## ⊘ ADVICE

● Prepare a detailed and useful kit before meeting the clients. Don't merely take the propaganda and brochure of your company and give them to the client. These materials will always be forgotten on the desk.

● For a meeting that many people will attend, it will be an excellent idea to provide a schedule or question list for the guests in advance. By doing this, everyone can communicate actively.

● In the West, a week begins with Sunday. But in China, it begins with Monday. If a western person says "last Monday" and "next Saturday" on Wednesday, he refers to "this week's Monday" and "this week's Saturday" respectively. But in China, "last Monday" and "next Saturday" refer to "last week's Monday" and "next week's Saturday." Remember this difference when discussing the meeting time.

# 送礼与受礼
## GIVING AND RECEIVING A GIFT

打开中国某购物网站，输入"礼物"，你可以得到 437 万余条商品信息，这些礼物价格不一、用途不一，送长辈、送老师、送客户、送领导、送孩子、送恋人，千姿百态。可见"礼"在中国人生活中的重要地位，以及礼物在建立和维护人际关系时起到的重要作用。

If you search "gift" on an online Chinese shopping website, you will get more than 4,370,000 results. These results cover a large variety of gifts with different prices and different usages, including those for elders, teachers, clients, leaders, children and lovers. It can be found that gifts play an important part in Chinese people's daily life. In addition, gifts also play an important role in building up and maintaining interpersonal relationships.

中国著名学者梁漱溟曾指出，中国社会更加看重个人之间的"关系"，而这种关系的构建和维系，很大一部分依赖于礼物的交换。"礼物"交换的是人与人之间的关系，同样交换的也是"人情"。"人情"像感情一样，是双方的事情，那么有"送礼"就要有"受礼"。《礼记·曲礼》中的"来而不往，非礼也"说的就是这个意思。

在中国，虽然有一句俗话叫"礼轻情意重"，但是礼物的轻重对感情的深浅还是有影响的。这是因为中国人将礼物交换和感情交流紧密地联系在一起，经常用礼物的价值来衡量"你对我是不是有感情"，或者"你是不是诚心诚意地想和我建立友谊"，所以中国人比较看重礼物的价值，也比较看重礼物的价值是否对等。比如，在商务活动中，如果你收到的礼物价值较高，那你回馈的礼物就不能只是一件小小的工艺品或其他小玩意儿。因为中国人重视的并非礼物和钱财，而是礼物背后价值所代表的"人情"、感情。

需要注意的是，礼物的价值需要对等，但不要送过于贵重的礼物。如果礼物过重，受礼者可能会担心自己成为人情的负债者，背上中国人常说的"人情债"，欠下人情债会在心中形成沉重的包袱。所以，如果受礼人说"无功不受禄"，那么他就是在坚持拒绝接受这份礼物，你就要再考虑一下，你送的礼物是否合适。

由于中国人看重的是礼物交换背后的情感交流，因此无论在送礼还是受礼的过程中，都表现得比较内敛。比如，中国人在送礼时，往往会说"小小礼物，不成敬意"，或者"我随便买的，也不知道你喜不喜欢"等等，但其实这礼物一定是送礼人精挑细选的。他之所以这样说，是因为不想让你因

The renowned Chinese scholar Liang Shuming once asserted that Chinese society lays more emphasis on "guanxi (interpersonal relationships)", and the establishment and maintenance of guanxi relies heavily on the exchange of gifts. When people exchange gifts, they are actually building up the relationship and doing favors for each other. They do favors for others and hope for favors in return. As the Summary of the Rules of Propriety (one chapter of *The Book of Rites*) says, "it's impolite not to make a return for what one receives". In other words, you should always remember to give a gift in return.

Although the Chinese saying goes "the gift itself may be small, but the goodwill is deep," people often attach great importance to the value of a gift and the equivalence of the gifts given by the two sides. The gift is closely related with the friendship, so Chinese people always measure your honesty and sincerity by the value of the gift. For example, if you receive an expensive gift, it would be impolite to give a small gift like a cheap handicraft in return. In fact, neither the gift nor the money matters, it is the favor or friendship it represents that really matters.

Besides, you should note that it is better not to give gifts that are too expensive. Large expensive gifts for individuals are best avoided because the Chinese will feel an obligation to repay the gift or the favor (known as "personal debt" in China), which could be a heavy burden. If the receiver says "wu gong bu shou lu (no gains without pains)", it means he refuses the gift resolutely. Maybe you should consider once again whether you chose the right gift or not.

To build an emotional connection with others, Chinese would show modesty and humility when giving and receiving gifts. For example, when giving a gift, a Chinese person will say "it's only a small gift" or "I just picked a gift for you, but don't know whether you will like it or not", but he doesn't really mean it. The gift is carefully selected. But to make you more comfortable to accept it, he will try to describe and present it as an inexpensive gift. Compared with him/her, the receiver will be more reserved. He/she will display his/her good self-control by not revealing visibly pleasure and also by not opening the gift immediately.

为礼物太贵重而有什么心理包袱。而受礼人的内敛会表现得更明显，受礼人往往不会喜形于色，更不会当面打开礼物，甚至有的人会推辞一番，说"哎呀，还带礼物干什么呀"，只有送礼人坚持两三次后才会收下。

当一个中国人收到礼物时，他可能即刻还礼。特别是在一些商务活动中，送礼和还礼几乎是同时进行的。这种时候最好事先作好调查，知道对方喜欢什么样的礼物，或者对方可能会送什么价位的礼物。而在较为私人的场合送了礼物，比如去中国人家里做客时送了礼物，中国人并不会立刻回礼，而是等一个适当的时机回礼。这样做是受礼人有意与送礼人维持一定的人际关系。如果即刻回礼，下次便难以找到联系的机会，而等一个适当的时机回礼，在这个一送一还的过程中便有了两次联系的机会，双方的联络也会更频繁。就像有人开玩笑说的，谈恋爱最好从借书开始，一借一还就能见两次面了，是一样的道理。

Sometimes, he might refuse the gift by saying "oh, you don't need to pick a gift for me" two or three times before accepting it.

If a Chinese person is offered a gift, he might give a gift in return immediately. It is very common to exchange gifts in some business activities. On these occasions, it is better to find out what gift the recipient might like in advance or to take a guess at the price of the gift given by him. If you give a gift during a more private occasion, such as a home visit, the Chinese host would find another proper time to repay your favor rather than at once on the spot. The reason is that he wants to maintain a relationship with you and be closer to you. If he offers a gift immediately, it would be difficult to find another chance to meet you again. To sum up, Chinese people always look forward to giving gifts in return as an opportunity to meet you face-to-face. Some people joke that borrowing a book from someone you fall in love with is the first step to start a relationship. It's the same as building up a relationship with the Chinese partners because you can meet the same person once again.

## 案例

　　Andre 初到中国工作，好客的中国同事老赵邀请他和其他同事去家里做客。Andre 问老赵是否需要带什么礼物，比如沙拉、红酒什么的。老赵爽快地说："你什么都不用带，自己来就可以了。" Andre 听了老赵的话，什么都没有带，如期赴约。结果其他同事都带了礼物，比如红酒、水果、给孩子的玩具、鲜花等等。Andre 两手空空站在门口，很尴尬。

　　**点评**　到中国人家中做客，最好带点儿小礼物，送什么礼物视你和主人的关系而定，鲜花、食物都可以。如果主人让你不要带礼物或者拒绝接收礼物，那往往是他们在与你客套，你坚持一下就好了。

## 行动指南

　　● 礼物不要用白色、黑色的包装，因为白色和黑色是丧葬时常用的颜色。

　　● 送礼不要送钟、伞、梨、菊花，因为"送钟"与"送终"谐音，"送伞"与"送丧"谐音，"梨"与 "离"谐音，表示分离，而菊花是中国人祭扫时常选的花儿。

　　● 如果到有小孩的同事家做客，不知道带什么礼物好，那不妨根据孩子的年龄准备一些玩具，一般都不会错。

## CASE STUDY

It is the first time for Andre to work in China. One day, his enthusiastic Chinese colleague Lao Zhao invited him and other colleagues to visit his home. Andre wanted to bring some gifts for Lao Zhao, so he asked him whether salads or wines are ok. "Don't bring any gift when you come," said Lao Zhao readily, so Andre didn't take anything that day. But when he arrived at the front door of Lao Zhao's home, he found every guest except him had brought a gift. They gave wines, fruits, toys (for Lao Zhao's children), flowers and other things to Lao Zhao. Standing in front of the door, Andre felt very embarrassed.

Comments: If invited to visit a Chinese home, you should take a small gift with you, such as flowers and food. You should take a gift even if the host told you not to. When you offer your gifts, you might experience a refusal. But it's only a Chinese courtesy, so you should persist and the host will finally accept it.

## ADVICE

● Never use white or black paper to wrap the gift up, as these two colors are traditionally associated with funerals.

● Certain items are better not given as gifts. These include watches or clocks, umbrellas, pearls and chrysanthemums. The Mandarin pronunciations of the phrase "give clock" and "give umbrella" share the same phonetic sound of the phrase "attend a funeral" and "take part in a funeral" respectively, which might imply death. The word "pearl" is pronounced the same as "leave", which means departing. Besides, chrysanthemums are only used for funerals in China.

● If you are going to visit a colleague with kids at his or her home, but don't know what gifts are suitable for the kids, in general, it would be a good idea to prepare some toys according to the age of the kids.

# 出差

## TRAVELING ON A
## BUSINESS TRIP

在中国出差，如果是中方安排行程，那你的出差行程可能会非常周到，周到得从早上睁开眼睛到晚上闭上眼睛每个时段都被安排得满满当当，被照顾得细致入微。

If you take a business trip in China and your schedule is arranged by the Chinese side, you can expect to have a very detailed arrangement. From the early morning when you get up until the night when you go to bed, they will arrange everything for you and look after you thoroughly.

中国人热情好客，特别是对远道而来的客人，机场落地有人接、一日三餐有人招待。如果你适应这种"被安排"的差旅，到中国出差是比较省心的。

在中国出差，如果你遇到了这种"被安排"的差旅，那么你会收到一份详尽的日程表。按照日程表的安排，早晨会有人带你去就餐，早餐很丰盛，有中式的也有西式的。早餐后会有人带你到工作地点或会议室，或是去参观企业。如果路程较远，一般都有专

车接送。会议所需的笔记本、笔、文件夹等办公文具一应俱全，甚至在此期间去卫生间都有人引导。

在中国出差，午餐即使是工作餐时间也有可能比较长，大家会相互敬酒、聊一些感兴趣的话题，甚至聊私生活，但是很少聊工作。晚上是差旅生活中的休闲时光，这时候接待方可

能会带你看一些有地方特色或民族特色的节目，尝尝当地的特色小吃，唱唱歌，喝喝酒等等。如果在出差期间遇到周末，那么这段时间将更加丰富多彩，可能会安排车程少于四个小时的本地旅游。

如果你在中国享受到了这样的待遇，不要奇怪，也不要不安。因为中国有个成语叫"宾至如归"，意思是客人来到这里就像回到自己家一样，接待方正是想为你营造一种"回家"的感觉。另外，接待方安排这些活动

还有一个目的，就是想和你建立较为亲密的私人关系，而建立亲密的私人关系往往是商务合作的开始。你也不妨利用这些机会，深入地了解一下你的合作伙伴。

结束了一天的工作和晚间的集体活动之后，接待方可能会私下找你，和你聊一聊合作的具体问题，或者和

It is a courtesy in China to meet visitors, especially those from afar, at the airport, and to greet and see them off by the door and arrange every meal for them. To some extent, if you are used to a visit in which everything is decided by the host, you will have a relaxing trip in China.

If the Chinese host arranges everything for you, a schedule in detail will be sent to you. Following the schedule, the contact person will take you to breakfast, usually a big breakfast with Chinese and western food. After that, you will be taken to the company or the conference room, or be guided to have a tour in the enterprise. If your hotel is far away from the company, the host will arrange a special car to pick you up and take you back. During the meeting, notebooks, pens, folders and other office accessories will be offered to you. There is even a person who will guide you to the restroom as necessary.

It is very likely that your lunch, even a business lunch, will last long in China. People will exchange toasts, talk about some events they are interested in and even their private life. But they will not talk much about business. When the sun goes down, the happiest time of the trip will come. The host may take you to watch some performances with local or ethnic features and enjoy some local snacks. He may also sing and drink alcohol with you and arrange other activities for you. On weekends, if you are in China, the host might arrange a local sightseeing trip for you. This experience will make your business trip more splendid.

If these things really occur, don't feel surprised and uneasy. As the Chinese four-character phrase "bin zhi ru gui" goes, the hosting party just wants to make you feel at home. The detailed arrangements are offered to establish a closer relationship with you since deep personal relationships are the key to starting a business between the two parties. Therefore, why not enjoy the trip and take this opportunity to get a better understanding of your potential partner?

After one day's work and all the activities, the host may get you in private to talk about the specific issues of the potential cooperation, or only to chat with you about hobbies or something you are interested in. You may have to sacrifice some private time to improve the

你聊聊天儿、谈谈兴趣爱好。这些都是增进感情的方式，并能由此建立较为亲密的私人关系。尽管会牺牲一些个人时间，但能为此后的商务活动做铺垫。

出差期间除了有接待方的热情招待，还会受到下属的周到照顾。在中国，如果你是年纪较长的领导，出差时年轻下属会对你关心有加，比如倒水、夹菜、办理酒店入住等等。但如果你是年轻的领导，随行下属与你同龄甚至比你年长，那么他们就不会那么细致入微地照顾你了。因为中国人注重上下等级，更注重长幼尊卑，讲究礼敬长者，对年龄大、辈分高的人给予特别的尊崇和敬重。早在《礼记》中就有"尚齿"、"序齿"、"齿让"等概念，这里的"齿"指的是"年龄"，表达了长幼有序、崇尚长者的意思。

在现代社会，尽管长幼尊卑的秩序不像古代那么森严，但还是会在日常生活中有所体现。如推崇"尊老爱幼"、给年长的人让座；又如商务活动中对位次的讲究——会议的位次、宴请的位次、乘车的位次等，甚至可能在上车、吃饭、进门出门之前，几个年纪、地位相当的人之间会相互谦让很久。

中国人注重长幼尊卑，却没有特别明确的性别优先习惯。现代中国人强调男女平等，人们一般不太习惯"女士优先"。不过随着国际化的不断影响，讲究"女士优先"的中国绅士越来越多了。

relationship between you and the host and finally be a close friend of him. But it's worthwhile to do so as the foundation of the business activities will be laid during the whole process.

If you were Chinese, besides the host, your subordinates will look after you thoroughly during the business trip. If you are an elder leader, the younger subordinates will arrange everything for you, such as preparing drinks, serving dishes, checking in the hotels and so on. If you are younger than or of the same age as your subordinates, such things won't occur anymore. Chinese society is hierarchical and a person's ranking counts for much. In China, it is a rule to respect those who are superior in society, which means that the elders and seniors should be respected. This rule can be found in the *The Book of Rites* (a collection of texts describing the social forms, administration, and ceremonial rites in ancient China). In the texts, the terms "shang chi", "xu chi" and "chi rang" all refer to the rule of respecting the senior. The term "chi" means "age".

In modern society, this rule is not as strict as that in ancient times, but people tend to obey it in daily life. For example, people consider it a social responsibility to respect aged and care for the young, and they encourage offering seats to elders. When doing business, there is a strict seating protocol in China: the seats of a meeting, banquet and vehicle will be arranged according to the ranking of the guests. What's more, when entering a car, having a meal and entering or going out from a door, the people of the same age and similar status will let others go first.

Although the rule of "filial piety" is obeyed by the Chinese, there is no clear gender priority in modern China. It is emphasized that men and women are equal nowadays. Generally speaking, Chinese people are not used to the rule of "lady first". But with the increasing influence of globalization, there are more and more gentlemen in China.

📖 **案例**

　　Mike 是就职于一家中国公司的外籍顾问。一天，Mike 在公司远远地看见秘书王小姐拎着一个大大的男士公文包，他很吃惊，怎么一个瘦弱的女孩子拎着这么大的包呢？还是男士的？ Mike 刚要上前帮忙，结果王小姐跟着张经理将公文包送到了经理办公室，原来是张经理的包。

　　Mike 吃惊地问同事小张："为什么在中国，女人给男人拿包？"小张大惊："不可能吧？" Mike 将事情的来龙去脉一说，小张才笑着说，原来是女下属给她的男上司拿包。可是 Mike 还是觉得不太理解。

📎 **点评**　在中国，在家人之间或亲友之间，男性会主动照顾女性，为女性拿东西、开门、打伞等。但在工作场合中，首先注重的是长幼秩序，其次是上下等级，最后可能才是性别。所以出现年轻女下属为年长男上司拿包的现象，就不奇怪了。

## 📖 CASE STUDY

Mike is a foreign consultant working in a Chinese company. One day, he saw the secretary Miss Wang carry a huge men's briefcase. Seeing such a thin girl carry a huge bag, Mike was very surprised. Before he went forward to help her, Wang took the briefcase to the manager's office. It turned out to be the manager's briefcase.

"Why Chinese woman help men to carry bags?" Mike asked his colleague Xiao Zhang with surprise. "How could it happen?" Xiao Zhang was astounded. Then Mike told the full story to him. Xiao Zhang realized that it was a female subordinate who carried her boss's bag, but he didn't know how to explain it to Mike.

✎ Comments: In China, among family members, relatives and friends, males take initiative to look after the females, such as by carrying things, opening doors and carrying umbrellas for them. But in the workplace, age ranks first, and rank or status comes second and gender ranks last. As a result, it is not surprising to see a young female subordinate carry the boss's bag.

## ⊙ 行动指南

- 中国的国土共跨越 5 个时区。自西向东依次是：东 5 区、东 6 区、东 7 区、东 8 区、东 9 区。目前，全中国统一采用北京时间，也就是东 8 区的区时。但由于中国跨越了 5 个时区，各地差距较大，有些地方会自行调整上下班的时间。比如地处中国西北部的新疆维吾尔自治区，由于日出时间较晚，上午和下午的上班时间通常分别是 10 点和 4 点，比北京地区的上班时间错后了整整两个小时。

- 中国从北到南分为 5 个温度带，分别是寒温带、中温带、暖温带、亚热带、热带，另外还有一个地高天寒、面积广大的高原气候区。因此，不同的城市，天气差别可能很大，比如海南省海口市气温高达 37℃，而同一天黑龙江省哈尔滨市的气温低达 -24℃—-12℃，两地最大温差超过 60℃。

## ⊘ ADVICE

● China geographically spans five time zones from west to east, namely, UTC+05:00, UTC+06:00, UTC+07:00, UTC+08:00 and UTC+09:00. Currently, in mainland China, standard time is called Beijing Time (UTC+08:00). Since China spans five time zones and there are big time differences, some places adjust working hour according to their own conditions. For instance, in the Xinjiang Uygur Autonomous Region, which is located in the northwest of China, the sun rise is quiet late based on Beijing Time. Therefore, working hours there start at 10:00 in the morning and at 4:00 in the afternoon, two hours later than that in Beijing.

● China has five temperature zones. From north to south, they are the frigid temperate zone, the medium temperate zone, the temperate zone, the subtropical zone and the tropical zone. In addition, there is a vast area capturing a plateau climate, where the oxygen is scarce and the temperature is low. The weather between different cities may also vary a lot. For example, when the average temperature of Haikou, Hainan province, reaches 37 ℃ , the temperature of Harbin in Heilongjiang province may be between- 24 ℃ and -12 ℃ . The maximum temperature difference between the two cities may reach 60℃ or more.

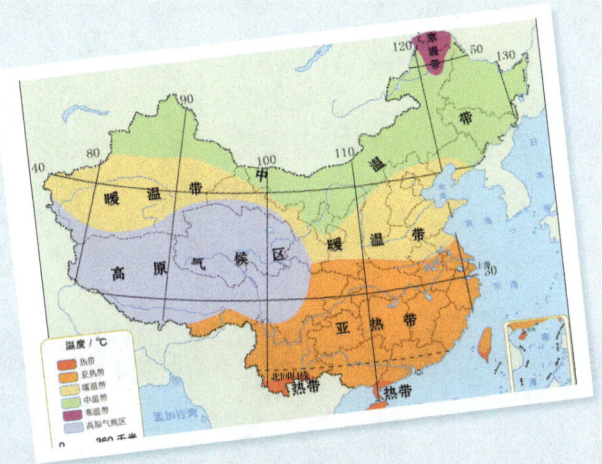

# 宴请
## DINING

中国有句古话叫"民以食为天"，饮食文化在中国占有很重要的地位，中国人也喜欢通过宴请的方式沟通、联络感情。在中国的宴会上有什么不一样的地方呢？

In China, there is an ancient saying, "hunger breeds discontentment". Since cuisine plays an essential role in China, people prefer to make social intercourse and friendly contacts through banquet settings. What are the differences between the Chinese banquets and western banquets?

中国有句话"和而不同"，人们崇尚和谐，但是允许有差别、鼓励多样化。这样的和谐在中国的宴会上也随处可见。

如果你去参加中国的宴会，入席的时候你最先注意到的或许就是餐桌，人们似乎对圆桌有着格外的偏爱，虽然也使用方桌，但那几乎是快餐店里专用的。圆桌旁的每个座位，没有固定的主宾、高低之分，人们依照座位与房间的位置、特别是大门的相对位置确定座位。这种浑然天成、一团和气的入座方式，正是中国人追求和谐的最好体现。

用餐的时候，中国人习惯聚餐制。菜肴会盛放在公用的盘子中，放在桌子中间，每个人面前只放自己的餐具。有的场合会准备公筷、公勺，供人们把菜夹到自己面前的餐具里，而更多的时候，人们会直接用各自的筷子从盘中夹取食物。有时桌大菜多，夹取食物多有不便，于是中国人发明了放在桌上可以转动的大玻璃盘，把菜肴放在上面，可以转到每个人面前。正是在不断转桌、让菜、布菜的过程中，人们的感情才能得到充分的交流。把刚上桌的菜转到某人面前，还能体现对他的尊重；及时发现宾客想吃哪道菜，并转到他的面前，更是能体现对客人的体贴。

The Chinese advocate "harmony in diversity", which means they strive for harmony but also uphold differences. This idea can usually be found in Chinese banquets.

When you attend a Chinese banquet, the first thing you may notice is the dining-table: it seems that the Chinese are in favor of the round table. Although square tables are used sometimes in a banquet, they are mainly used by fastfood restaurants. Every seat around the round table is equal. These seats are arranged according to the direction of the room (mainly the location of the door) instead of status or ranking. This is the best embodiment of the harmony that Chinese people desired for.

In China, people like to eat together, which means that the dishes are put on the center of the table and shared by all people. Personal tableware is put in front of each person. In some cases, communal chopsticks and spoons may be offered. However, in most cases, people are used to using their own chopsticks to pick up food. Sometimes, it's inconvenient to reach the food by a large table with so many dishes. To solve this problem, the wise Chinese created the Lazy Susan tabletop which is put on the center of the table. People can pick up every dish by turning the Lazy Susan. By continuously turning the tabletop, and serving food to each other, the guests and host get into deep communication with each other. It's a good way to express your respect to people by serving a new dish to them. Besides, when you notice that somebody wants to eat a particular food, it would be very kind of you to turn the Lazy Susan to help him/her get it.

The Chinese also focus on harmony when choosing tableware. They are very good at using two thin sticks skillfully, but cutlery with points or blades are not used during meals. A piece of cutlery with point or blade is considered as a symbol of violence. Compared with them, chopsticks look safer. It's rude to "choke" food with chopsticks or insert them into dishes. It is believed by the Chinese that "food is never too refined to eat". So they spend a huge amount of time preparing the food, and no matter how complicated the process is, it should only be done in the kitchen. It is not allowed to cut and chop food on the dinner tables.

中国人在餐具的使用上非常注重和谐。中国人善于平衡、运作两支独立的筷子，在餐桌上不使用有尖或刃的餐具。尖和刃总显得剑拔弩张，筷子却是柔和的。并且也只能用"夹"这种柔和的动作，如果用筷子插、戳食物，也会被认为是不雅的。中国人讲究"食不厌精，脍不厌细"，但再复杂的加工工作，也只能在厨房里完成，切菜、切肉的动作是不许出现在餐桌上的。"君子远庖厨"，一方面是因为见动物生而不忍食其肉，另一方面，也是因为吃饭是和谐的事，不宜操刀。

在菜品选择和烹饪方面，和谐也是很重要的。不同场合下，菜肴有丰俭之别，但荤素、冷热搭配都是要讲究的，整桌宴席一定要协调。中国菜也很少只用一种原料做，即使以某种食材为主，通常也要放配菜或点缀，比如翠绿的菜叶或青椒、鲜红的胡萝卜或红椒，甚至盘边精心雕刻的一朵萝卜花儿——它在这里并非是一种食物，而仅仅是一个点缀，满足视觉上的美观和平衡。

如果你在不同的城市吃同样名字的菜，而它们的口味大相径庭，请不要吃惊，更无需责问厨师是否用

There is an old saying in China that "gentleman should be far away from the kitchen". This is partly because gentlemen think it's too crude to see uncooked meat. The other reason is that seeing the cutlery with sharp blades may ruin the harmonious atmosphere of eating.

When choosing and cooking dishes, harmony is also very important. The quality and amount of the dishes may vary as the situation changes, but no matter how simple a meal is, it should be well-balanced. The hot and cold dishes with meat and vegetables should be served. The Chinese dishes always consist of a number of different ingredients cooked together. Even if a dish mainly consists of one ingredient, side dishes or vegetables such as green peppers, red pepper, red carrot and even a floriated radish (put at the edge of the plate) are often served as decorations. These vegetables are not offered to eat but to create a visual feast for the guests.

Don't feel surprised when you find the dishes with the same name tasting different in different cities. You don't need to doubt whether the chef is unprofessional. The reason is that Chinese people from different regions prefer to create new flavors and new ways of cooking rather than have the same flavor. For example, if you order a dish, it may be more salty in Shandong, sweeter in Guangdong and spicier in Sichuan. Different flavors are always welcomed by the Chinese.

Besides proper seating arrangement and various dishes, the harmonious atmosphere is also important in a banquet. To make the guests feel warm and welcome, the host will keep toasting, breaking into dishes, serving food to the guests and insisting that they should eat more. Moreover, to create a harmonious atmosphere, Chinese people usually regard the host and guests as a team. The guests are the members of the team, while the host is the head. Therefore, it's the host's duty and right to cheer the guests up and help them eat more and drink more. The guests are supposed to follow the arrangement of the host. Although people of increasing numbers are pursuing personality and freedom, most of the time they may think it is a good way to show intimacy by making decisions for the guests as long as the host is sincere in it.

心——恰恰相反，中国人并不强求各地口味一致，而是更乐于开发新口味、新做法。同样一道菜，在山东地区可能偏咸鲜，在广东偏甜淡，在四川偏麻辣……中国人向来乐于包容不同的口味。

有这样和谐的座位安排、丰富的菜品，中国人当然希望客人吃饭时，也能热闹、融洽、尽兴。为了实现这种气氛，人们习惯不断为客人敬酒、让菜、布菜，陪客人聊天儿，觉得这样才尽东道之谊。由于人们追求和谐融洽的氛围，便把一起吃饭的人看做一个集体，而客人则是"自己人"，作为集体的一分子、氛围的主导者，主人有责任也有权利调节气氛、招呼客人多吃多喝，客人也该"客随主便"，尽量听从主人安排。尽管如今越来越推崇个性与自由，多数中国人仍觉得，如果是"为了你好"，那么替人做主就并非是干涉他人的选择，而是亲密关系的体现。

自然，客人们吃得越多、喝得越爽快，主人就越高兴。可是如果你把桌上的菜吃得一点儿不剩（实际上在中国人的餐桌上这点很难做到），主人却会担忧了：是否准备的饭菜太少？有没有让客人饿肚子？会不会让客人觉得自己小气？请客吃饭，吃的其实不是"饭"，而是气氛和排场，食物越丰盛，丰盛到让客人大快朵颐后还能剩下一些，越能体现主人的大方和对客人的重视。

主人准备得隆重，招待得热情，客人吃得爽快，席间气氛热闹，无疑是对主宾关系的促进，如果以后要谈生意，多半都会顺利。甚至有很多关键决定，其实都不是在谈判桌上，而是在酒桌上定下来的。宴席不仅是最容易发现中国人性格的场合，更是最容易跟中国人建立关系、拉近距离的地方。

The more the guests eat and drink, the happier the host will be. However, if no food is left, the host may start to worry that the food is not enough. He may begin to wonder whether the guests are hungry or whether he looks like a stingy host to them. Chinese people are usually prudent in their daily life, but they prefer to host a lavish banquet for the guests. In fact, the atmosphere and the amount of the food are more important than the food itself. For the Chinese, the more the dishes are, the more generous and sincere the host is. After an all-you-can-eat meal, if there is still something left on the plates, the host may feel comfortable.

By making an impressive welcome ceremony and banquet, as well as showing great hospitality, the guests will be satisfied during the visit. During the meal, the host and guests will get much closer, which would promote future cooperation between the two sides. You can note that many important decisions are not made in the negotiations, but on the dinner-tables. Banquets are a good opportunity to learn about Chinese culture and Chinese people's personality. More importantly, it is the best chance to build a close relationship with the Chinese during a meal.

📖 **案例**

　　Alan 和同事第一次在中国赴宴，主人一直热情地替他们夹菜，饭菜味道不错，Alan 他们吃了很多。谁知看到饭菜不多了，主人竟然又添了几个菜。但是 Alan 和同事们已经吃不下了，看着剩下的半桌菜，Alan 有点儿尴尬，没想到主人反而很满意。

✎**点评**　中国人认为，为客人准备丰盛的酒席才是待客之道。如果一顿饭吃到最后一点儿不剩，则会担心客人是否吃饱、是否觉得受到慢待。不过，现在中国人也越来越讲究节约，不会再准备太过量的饭菜了。如果你实在吃不下，不用硬撑，如实相告就可以，主人绝不会为此不开心。

**CASE STUDY**

It was the first time that Alan and his colleagues attended a banquet in China. To show great hospitality, the host kept putting food on their plates. The food was so tasty that they ate quite a lot. Finding out the food may be not enough, the host ordered more dishes for them. However, Alan and his colleagues were already full. Leaving over so much food on the table, they felt very embarrassed but the host was very happy to see that.

Comments: In China, people usually prepare more food than the guests really need in order to show their hospitality and respect for the guests. If all the food is finished, the host may wonder why they didn't provide enough food to feed the guests. However, with growing awareness of the "thrifty concept", Chinese people are not preparing excessive food to serve guests nowadays. If you really feel very full, just tell the host honestly. He will not be unhappy about that.

**⊘ 行动指南**

- 在中餐桌上，一般摆放着这些餐具：

  ➢ 自用餐具：

汤匙
碗
碟子
筷子

茶杯
喝红酒的高脚杯
喝白酒的小酒杯

  ➢ 公用餐具（供人们之间互相布菜用）：

    勺子，筷子。

- 中国宴会比较讲究座次。在正式的宴会上，客人最好听主人的安排入座，而家宴的座位安排则相对随意。

- 中国宴会有一定的上菜顺序，一般是先上冷盘，再上热菜，最后是汤和主食，有些地方还有甜点或果盘。

- 如果主人不断地为你布菜，有的可能是你不喜欢吃的，你可以留一点儿菜在盘子里，主人再次布菜的时候，可以以"盘子里还有"为理由委婉地拒绝主人的好意。

- 不要把筷子插在饭碗里，否则会让人联想到祭祀，不吉利。

- 在中国东南沿海城市，比如广东、香港、福建等地，吃鱼的时候不可以把鱼翻面。这些地方的人们会觉得把鱼翻过来象征着翻船，很不吉利。

## ⊘ ADVICE

- The following tableware is often seen on the dinner-table:

  ➢ Personal tableware:

  Spoons, bowls, plates, chopsticks, tea cups, goblets for red wine, and glasses for liquor.

  ➢ Communal tableware :

  Spoons and chopsticks offered to serve food for others.

- People pay great attention to the arrangement of the seats in a banquet. In formal situations, it would be polite to follow the host's arrangement. However, people may sit where they like in a family visit.

- Dishes are usually served in a certain order. Cold dishes are served first, followed by hot dishes, soups and staple food. Desserts and fruits may be provided at the end of the meal sometimes.

- If you find your host starts putting food on your plate, do not reject it even if you don't like the food. It would be a good idea to leave a little food on your plate to dissuade the host politely.

- Don't insert your chopsticks vertically into your bowl. Chinese people only do that when they offer sacrifices to gods or ancestors.

- In the coastal regions in the southeast of China, such as Guangdong, Hong Kong and Fujian, it is not allowed to turn over a fish during the meal because it's an unlucky act which means that someone's boat may be capsized.

# 饮酒
## DRINKING

中国有句话叫"无酒不成席"，酒在宴席上占有重要地位。为什么中国人如此重视酒呢？

As a Chinese saying goes, "there's no feast without alcohol". Alcohol plays a very important role in feasts. But why do Chinese people pay so much attention to alcohol?

中国人重视酒，并非因为对酒本身有特别的偏爱（在简单的日常三餐中酒并非必需），酒的重要性在于，在交际宴会上可以活跃气氛，有助于联络感情，能够让宴会很容易地变得和谐而热闹。

有句俗话是"酒后吐真言"，人们愿意相信喝酒之后的交流更坦诚。当然，一旦有了这个意识，可能不需要喝到大醉或微醺，仅仅有一点儿象征性的酒精摄入和气氛的烘托，人们就能放松下来，展开坦诚而热烈的交流。所以，在宴席上，很多本来不苟言笑的人，常常在喝酒之后就开始推杯换盏、谈笑风生了。

在拉近人际距离这一点上，烟跟酒的作用很相似，因此也有"烟酒不分家"的说法。在中国，与陌生人随意搭讪聊天儿不太常见，但如果跟正在吸烟的陌生人借个火儿，却不会有何不妥，也不用担心被拒绝。跟酒一样，香烟也能在无形之中拉近人们的心理距离。

宴会上，不止有开场的祝酒，人们还会反复地举杯、敬酒，不光是全体一起干杯，还要有单独的敬酒，敬酒也可能不止一轮，有些地区甚至讲究每轮敬酒都要喝两三次。如果到了少数民族地区，敬酒可能更为郑重。比如蒙古族人敬酒时，主人会献上哈达（表示敬意或庆祝的长丝巾），并唱起祝酒歌，客人接过酒杯要先用无名指沾一滴向上洒表示敬天，沾一滴向下洒表示敬地，再沾一滴点自己的额头表示敬祖先。如果客人能将杯中酒一饮而尽，主人

Alcohol is not the most preferred drink for Chinese people (daily meals are not always accompanied by alcohol), but it is very important during the meal. The alcohol would make the party more lively, help friendly communication and create a harmonious atmosphere.

A Chinese proverb says that "truth comes with the alcohol." People tend to believe that communication could be more sincere and frank after drinking. With this saying in mind, people could only relax and talk warmly and frankly to each other by drinking a little alcohol in a friendly atmosphere. Thus, many people, who may not enjoy talking before, often could not stop talking and joking after having alcohol drinks.

To shorten the distance between the two parties, cigarettes have the same effect as alcohol does. That's why people say "cigarettes and alcohol are the members of one family." In China, it is not common for a person to initiate a chat with a stranger. However, it is very common to borrow a lighter from a stranger without worrying one will be refused. As the alcohols, cigarettes can also make people closer though they may not be aware of that.

The starting toast is generally followed by several rounds of toasts proposed for a variety of best wishes. The toasts may take place all together and may be proposed between two persons. In some regions, sometimes, one round of toast may include several bottom-ups. In ethnic minority regions, toasting may be accompanied by other ceremonies. Mongolian people, for example, always offer guest a Khata (a scarf made of silk) and sing special toasting songs when proposing a toast. In response to the toast, the guest should take the glass and touch the alcohol inside with ring finger. Then, the guest should throw one drop upwards to show

会很高兴；如果客人不会喝酒也不必勉强，可以沾唇示意，表示接受了主人纯洁的情谊。现在，在城市里，这样传统的敬酒仪式逐渐简化，但敬酒的习惯依旧。

有人认为能喝酒，特别是喝光别人敬的酒，是一个人随和、有诚意、乐于合作的表现。尤其是在北方或少数民族地区，人们喜欢把杯中的酒一次喝光。这也就使得有些人会习惯性地劝酒、不自觉地灌酒、喝多，也就有"喝倒才能喝好"的说法了。现在这样的想法正在逐渐改变，敬酒的人越来越多地说"随意"，意思是大家可以根据自己的意愿饮酒，想喝多少就喝多少。

一般来说，在中国的酒桌上，最重要的酒是白酒，这是中国最传统的酒精饮料之一；另一种是黄酒，在南方更为常见；随着时代的发展，现在啤酒、红酒在酒桌上也很常见。在中国的酒桌上，虽然酒必不可少，但也允许不喝酒的人（尤其是女士）用其他饮料来替代酒，如果汁等软饮料、茶水，甚至是白水，所以有"以茶代酒"、"以水代酒"等说法。因为最重要的还是气氛，而非酒本身，而人们的习惯也正在改变，"喝好"并非总意味着要"喝倒"了。所以，如果你真的不喝酒，也不要破坏酒桌上的氛围，在大家干杯、敬酒的时候，可以用其他饮料一同举杯。

the respect to heaven, throw one downwards to the earth, and one at his own forehead for the ancestors. The host would be delighted if the guest could bottom up the glass of alcohol. But, it is not necessary for a teetotaler —the guest can sip a little to accept the hospitality and sincerity of the host. Nowadays the traditional toasting ceremony has been simplified in the cities, but the toasting tradition still remains.

It is believed in general that those who bottom up the alcohol are easy going and willing to cooperate. People in northern China or some ethnic minority regions are used to bottoming up the glass of alcohol. Proposing toast followed by drinking too much produces one saying: "getting drunk makes you enjoy the drinking". Nowadays, the way of drinking is changing gradually. It is more often for people to say, "Let's please ourselves on that". It means that you could enjoy drinking no matter how much you drink.

Generally speaking, Baijiu (liquor) is the most important alcohol at the feast. It is also one of the most traditional and common alcohols in China. Huangjiu (yellow rice wine) is more popular in South China. With the development of the society, now beers and wines are often seen at the feast. It is true that alcohol is necessary at a feast, but people who don't drink alcohol (ladies in most cases) are allowed to have soft drinks, such as juice, tea and water. In these instances can be heard the phrases "drink tea as alcohol" or "drink water as alcohol". It is the atmosphere, rather than the alcohol, that plays the most important part in the banquet. But things are changing now: "enjoy yourself with alcohols" doesn't necessarily mean "getting drunk". But you should note that if you are a teetotaler, try not refusing others' toasting. And when the toasting begins, you should raise your glass filled with a soft drink instead of alcohol.

## 📖 案例

　　Brain 是中国南方 A 公司的经理,因业务往来到中国北方拜访 B 公司。Brain 是第一次上门,B 公司为他举行了隆重的欢迎宴会。 Brain 发现,这里的人们酒量很大,而且喝的都是白酒。宴会上,接待方热情地劝酒,气氛很热烈,Brain 平时不喝酒,这次实在盛情难却,几杯白酒下肚,Brain 已酩酊大醉了。

📝 **点评**　在中国,不同的地方喝酒的习惯也不太一样,总的来说,都很重视饮酒,中国北方和少数民族地区尤其重视。如果你真的不擅饮酒,不妨提前告诉主人,给你上度数低一点儿的酒或者其他饮料,他们会理解的。

## ⊙ 行动指南

　　● 中国人碰杯时说的"干杯",原本不仅仅是一句套话,而是真的要"干了杯里的酒"。有时,为了表示杯中的酒真的干了,还会把杯口亮出来。现在往往被用作碰杯时的表示,但如果对方喝干了杯里的酒,你最好也一样喝干。

　　● 赴中国宴会时,如果你不喝酒,那就一滴都不要喝,如果喝了,就请作好喝更多的准备。

　　● 如果要敬酒,那就应该把桌上的每个人都敬到。因为敬酒是表示一种问候,跳过任何一个人都是不礼貌的。

## 📰 CASE STUDY

Brain is the manager of Company A in southern China. He visited Company B in northern China for business one day. It was his first visit to that company, so the host held a grand welcome banquet for him. Brain found everyone except him could drink a large amount of Baijiu (liquor). During the banquet, the atmosphere was great, and the host toasted Brain and urged him to drink. Brain didn't drink actually, but this time, he found it difficult to reject the toasts. Finally, he drank several glasses of liquor and was dead drunk.

🔖 Comments: In China, people from different regions have different customs of drinking. Generally speaking, they all pay great attention to drinking, especially those from northern China and ethnic minority regions. If you can't drink much, the host will understand if you tell him in advance. They can serve you wine with low alcoholic content or soft drinks.

## ⊘ ADVICE

• When Chinese people say *ganbei* ("bottoms up") while toasting, it really means that you should empty the glass in one swallow. Sometimes, people may show out the edge of glass to tell others that the glass is empty.

• When attending a banquet or feast in China, don't drink alcohol if you are a teetotaler. If you sip some, you should be prepared to drink much.

• If you want to raise a toast, you should toast everyone at your table. Toasting is regarded as a greeting in China, so it's not polite to miss anyone.

图书在版编目 (CIP) 数据

商务活动 /《中国商务文化》编写组编著. —北京 : 北京语言大学出版社，2013.12（2016.12 重印）
　　（中国商务文化）
　　ISBN 978-7-5619-3712-9

Ⅰ . ①商⋯　Ⅱ . ①中⋯　Ⅲ . ①商务 – 活动　Ⅳ . ①F715

中国版本图书馆CIP数据核字（2013）第295323号

| 书　　名： | 商务活动 |
| --- | --- |
| | SHANGWU HUODONG |
| 责任编辑： | 王墨妍 |
| 责任印制： | 陈　辉 |

| 出版发行： | 北京语言大学出版社 |
| --- | --- |
| 社　　址： | 北京市海淀区学院路15号　　邮政编码：100083 |
| 网　　址： | www.blcup.com |
| 电　　话： | 编辑部　　8610-8230 1016 |
| | 国内发行　8610-8230 3650/3591/3648 |
| | 海外发行　8610-8230 0309/3365/3080 |
| | 读者服务部　8610-8230 3653 |
| | 网上订购电话　8610-8230 3908 |
| | 客户服务信箱　service@blcup.com |
| 印　　刷： | 北京建宏印刷有限公司 |
| 经　　销： | 全国新华书店 |

| 版　　次： | 2014年1月第1版　　2016年12月第3次印刷 |
| --- | --- |
| 开　　本： | 889毫米×1194毫米　　1/16　　印张：5.25 |
| 字　　数： | 86千字 |
| 书　　号： | ISBN 978-7-5619-3712-9 / F・13301 |
| 定　　价： | 196.00元（含DVD） |

凡有印装质量问题，本社出版部负责调换。电话：010–82303590

Printed in China